John Paul Jones

Father of the U.S. Navy

Colonial Leaders

Lord Baltimore *English Politician and Colonist*

Benjamin Banneker *American Mathematician and Astronomer*

William Bradford *Governor of Plymouth Colony*

Benjamin Franklin *American Statesman, Scientist, and Writer*

Anne Hutchinson *Religious Leader*

Cotton Mather *Author, Clergyman, and Scholar*

William Penn *Founder of Democracy*

John Smith *English Explorer and Colonist*

Miles Standish *Plymouth Colony Leader*

Peter Stuyvesant *Dutch Military Leader*

Revolutionary War Leaders

Benedict Arnold *Traitor to the Cause*

Nathan Hale *Revolutionary Hero*

Alexander Hamilton *First U.S. Secretary of the Treasury*

Patrick Henry *American Statesman and Speaker*

Thomas Jefferson *Author of the Declaration of Independence*

John Paul Jones *Father of the U.S. Navy*

Thomas Paine *Political Writer*

Paul Revere *American Patriot*

Betsy Ross *American Patriot*

George Washington *First U.S. President*

Revolutionary War Leaders

John Paul Jones

Father of the U.S. Navy

Norma Jean Lutz

Arthur M. Schlesinger, jr.
Senior Consulting Editor

Chelsea House Publishers

Philadelphia

Dedication: To Elliott Eastburn, with love from your great aunt

Produced by 21st Century Publishing and Communications, Inc.
New York, NY. http://www.21cpc.com

CHELSEA HOUSE PUBLISHERS
Editor in Chief Stephen Reginald
Production Manager Pamela Loos
Director of Photography Judy L. Hasday
Art Director Sara Davis
Managing Editor James D. Gallagher

Staff for *JOHN PAUL JONES*
Project Editor/Publishing Coordinator Jim McAvoy
Associate Art Director Takeshi Takahashi
Series Design Keith Trego

The Chelsea House World Wide Web address is
http://www.chelseahouse.com

First Printing
1 3 5 7 9 8 6 4 2

Library of Congress Cataloging-in-Publication Data

Lutz, Norma Jean.
John Paul Jones / by Norma Jean Lutz.
80 pp. cm. — (Revolutionary War Leaders series)
Includes bibliographical references and index.
Summary: A biography of the well-known naval leader, John Paul
Jones, from his birth in Scotland through his participation in the
American Revolution to his death in Paris at the age of forty-five.
ISBN 0-7910-5359-8 (hc)   ISBN 0-7910-5702-X (pb)
1. Jones, John Paul, 1747-1792—Juvenile literature. 2. Admirals—
United States—Biography—Juvenile literature. 3. United States
Navy—Biography—Juvenile literature. 4. United States—History—
Revolution, 1775-1783—Naval operations—Juvenile literature.
[1. Jones, John Paul, 1747-1792. 2. Admirals. 3. United States—
History—Revolution, 1775-1783—Biography.] I. Title. II. Series.
E207.J7L85   1999
973.3'5'092—dc21   99-25051
[B]   CIP

Publisher's Note: In Colonial and Revolutionary War America, there were no standard rules for spelling, punctuation, capitalization, or grammar. Some of the quotations that appear in the Colonial Leaders and Revolutionary War Leaders series come from original documents and letters written during this time in history. Original quotations reflect writing inconsistencies of the period.

Contents

A small town on a bay in the 1700s. Growing up near the water in Scotland, John Paul Jones spent many hours watching the ships come and go with their goods on Solway Firth.

A Young Scottish Sailor

The greatest American naval hero in history was born on July 6, 1747, in a small cottage in Scotland to a family by the name of Paul. The infant child was named John Paul after his father. The name Jones was not added until many years later.

This cottage was located on the large estate of Arbigland. John's father was head gardener for the estate. That meant that he was in charge of all the workers who took care of the herb and vegetable gardens, the grand and beautiful flower beds, and the many fruit orchards.

Solway Firth is a bay that juts far inland just

between Britain and Scotland, nearly cutting the island in half. Arbigland lay near Solway Firth. As a boy, John spent many hours at the bay and watched in fascination as all manner of ships carried their goods to the nearby towns of Kirkcudbright (pronounced "Kirkoobry") and Dumfries.

John was fourth in a family of five children— he had an older brother, William, and three sisters, Elizabeth, Janet, and Mary Ann. While the stone cottage may have been crowded with so many children, there was never any lack of food. Scottish gardeners always had the right to all the milk and vegetables their families could eat. In addition to fruits and vegetables, John grew up eating large bowls of porridge made from home-ground oatmeal, meat stews, and an endless supply of salmon taken from the nearby Solway.

Just a mile or so from Arbigland was the Kirkbean parish church where the Paul family attended services each week. When he was old

**Ships being loaded in a harbor town.
As a boy, John played on the docks and
heard exciting stories of life at sea.**

enough, John attended the church's elementary
school. His teacher, Reverend James Hogg,
must have been a good schoolmaster because
John Paul learned how to express himself well
in writing.

In 1756, when John was nine, his older brother William sailed to America. There he opened a tailor shop in Fredericksburg, Virginia. Letters from William told the family about the new freedoms to be found in America. William also explained in the letters about the growing anger of the colonists against the British rulers.

Gardening was not of great interest to John. Ships, boats, and water were what interested the Scottish lad. John and his playmates spent hours sailing toy ships along the sandy shores of the River Nith, which spilled into the Solway. John was often the leader of the boys, shouting commands to the imaginary fleet. The boys knew how to handle rowboats and small sail-boats because water was the best mode of travel at that time.

At the nearby port town of Carsethorn, John played on the ships at the docks and listened as the old sailors told him wild tales of adventures at sea. They taught him to speak in different languages and showed him how to tie knots. It was no surprise to anyone that when John was old enough to become an **apprentice** and learn a trade, he chose to go to sea.

Had John belonged to a wealthy family with enough money and the right connections, he might have become a midshipman in the Royal Navy. However, all John had were neighbors who knew a ship owner named James Younger. Younger lived in the British town of Whitehaven across the Solway Firth.

When he was only 13 years old, John left Arbigland aboard a small fishing vessel that carried him to Whitehaven. There he signed on to be an apprentice for Mr. Younger for seven years. He would earn very little money but would learn to be a worthy seaman.

John's first voyage was on the ship, or **brig**, named *Friendship,* which was first sailing to Barbados and then on to America. The brig carried a crew of 28 along with 18 guns. A brig like the *Friendship* had two masts and many sails. Each sail was controlled by ropes called running rigging. This is where John's rope-tying skills would serve him well. Aboard the ship he would learn each of the riggings and how to handle them.

The life of a seaman's apprentice was not an easy one. While the captain and the officers slept in cabins in the **stern**, or the back, of the boat, the other crew slept in crowded conditions in the **bow**, or front of the boat. With no other place left for John, he slept in a swinging hammock that had to be rolled up and put away each morning.

His duties probably included scrubbing and scraping the decks, cleaning out the living quarters, and emptying garbage. He may have also helped the cook in the galley by washing out pots and pans and carrying water. All crew members were always expected to obey orders. Those who did not were severely punished. If the offense was serious enough, the guilty person might receive a flogging (a beating using a rod or a whip).

A British label advertising Virginia tobacco. John's first job was on a ship that carried tobacco and other items.

The *Friendship* landed in Barbados and unloaded its cargo of wool and butter. After being reloaded with rum and sugar, it sailed toward Virginia, where that cargo was sold. The ship then took on tobacco, **pig iron**, and

A British cartoon of hard-working American colonists. After a visit to his brother in America, John wanted to settle there and make his fortune.

barrel staves to sell back in Britain. The *Friendship,* with John as a crew member, would make four such round trips in the next few years, buying and selling goods.

John was fortunate in that he was able to stay several days with his brother, William, while in Virginia. There he met people who were refined and cultured. William Paul had met people such as George Washington's sister Betty and her husband, Fielding Lewis. The Lewises lived in a beautiful house with fine furniture imported from Britain.

This made an impression on John, and he later made the decision not to socialize or mix with "low company" in his travels. He would instead seek out gentlemen and ladies. He worked at getting rid of his strong accent or Scottish **brogue**. Whatever free time he had, he spent reading good books.

In later years he would say that he fell in love with America at first sight. He wished he would someday call it his home. Although he would later live and spend time in his adopted homeland, he never actually made a permanent life in America.

In 1764 Mr. Younger's shipping company went out of business. John was released from his apprenticeship. He would have to search for a new way to make a living at sea.

A map of the West Indies. John worked on ships from Jamaica and Tobago before trouble forced him to leave the islands and move to Virginia.

Trouble in Tobago

John Paul wanted to make enough money so that one day he could buy land in America and settle there. The quickest way to make a lot of money in the 1760s was to be a slave trader. John signed on as third mate on another ship, the *King George*. The *King George* picked up slaves in West Africa and sold them in the West Indies. Slaves were packed into the hold of the ships as compactly as possible. Many of them died during the voyage.

From ships' records we know that John served on the *King George* for at least two years, then became chief officer on the *Two Friends*. This 30-ton ship was

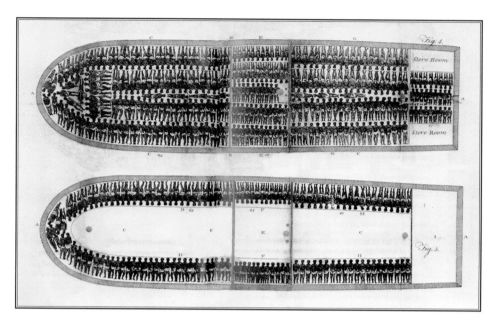

**Diagrams show the placement of slaves in the hold
of a ship on the way from Africa. Many slaves died
on the trip because of the harsh conditions.**

smaller, not even 50 feet long. With the crew
plus 77 slaves squeezed aboard, it must have
been a terrible trip. When the *Two Friends*
docked in Kingston, Jamaica, John had had
enough. He called slave trading an "abominable
trade" and quit right then and there. John never
worked in the slave business again.

On July 6, 1768, a brig called *John* docked
in Kingston. John knew the ship's master, whose

name was McAdam. Mr. McAdam happened to be from Kirkcudbright and he offered John free passage home if John wanted it. John accepted. On the way back to Scotland, McAdam and the first mate both died of a fever. Since John was the only one left onboard who knew how to navigate the ocean, he took over and brought the ship safely home. The owners of the ship were so thankful that they appointed John the new master. At the age of 21 John became captain of his own vessel.

While other men as young or younger than John were in command of seagoing vessels, they were usually sons of the captains or sons of owners of shipping companies. John, on the other hand, had no family influence to help him along. He worked hard for his promotions.

As a captain, John was a very strict leader. Because he was young and small, he felt he had to be hard on his men to establish strong leadership. His crew members nicknamed him a "dandy skipper" because he dressed more like a naval officer than a merchant seaman.

On a voyage to the Windward Islands, John became angry at a crew member named Mungo Maxwell. John had Maxwell tied up and lashed with a **cat-o'-nine-tails**. When the ship arrived in Tobago, Maxwell filed a complaint. The judge ruled in favor of the captain, saying the lashing was "neither mortal nor dangerous."

Maxwell took another vessel homeward and died of a fever on the way. But Maxwell's father decided that his son had died from the flogging. When John arrived home in Scotland, he was promptly arrested and put in a local prison. Fortunately, he was able to raise bail and be released. He wasted no time in sailing back to the West Indies to obtain proof of his innocence. Statements from the judge, as well as from others, helped to clear John's name. However, the story that he flogged a man to death followed him for many years.

It was during this time that John was accepted into a secret club called the Freemasons. The

Freemasons are a group of men who meet and have secret ceremonies and oaths that bind them together. As a member of the group in Kirkcudbright, John would also be welcomed in any other Freemason's group, whether it was in France or America or Britain. This helped him to make important contacts later in life.

When the owners of the *John* sold the ship in 1771, they gave John high recommendations. They said he was a good tradesman and a good ship captain.

In October 1772 John became captain of a square-rigged ship, the *Betsy*. He may have even been part owner. By going into partnership with a merchant on the island of Tobago, John was becoming wealthy. He still hoped to become a gentleman farmer in Virginia. A single event, however, changed those plans forever.

The *Betsy* had arrived in Tobago. Several crew members had families on the island and needed money. The crew demanded their wages in advance, which was unusual. John had planned on holding his cash to invest in cargo and then paying the men upon return to Britain.

One crew member was more determined than the rest. John later referred to him as the "ringleader." John attempted to calm the men by offering them clothing, but the ringleader refused the gift. The ringleader began lowering one of the small boats to go ashore without permission. John took up his sword and ordered the man to stop. Instead of frightening him, this made the man even more angry. He came at John with a club. John charged forward, running into the man with his sword and killing him.

History is not clear exactly why John fled the island. We do know that he first turned himself in to a justice of the peace. But the justice of the peace advised him that wasn't necessary until he was ready to stand trial. At that point his friends must have warned him that anger among the local citizens put him in danger. His friends told him to leave quickly. John rode by horseback to the opposite side of the island where another ship was ready to leave. He left all his affairs and property and took only 50 pounds (British money) with him. When he registered on the ship he wrote the name John Jones.

The next few months of John's life are a mystery. Even in later letters, he never revealed where he had been or what he had done. His name change makes it difficult to trace his whereabouts.

John Jones, as he was now known, showed up in Virginia in 1774. His brother William had died the year before but left no money or property to either his brother or his wife. John was befriended, possibly through the Freemasons group, by Dr. John K. Read. Dr. Read was a nephew of Benjamin Franklin's wife.

In 1775 John went to Philadelphia, and there he became acquainted with Joseph Hewes, a delegate to the Second Continental Congress. He also came in contact with Thomas Jefferson, who was a close friend to Dr. Read. John knew the colonists' anger against Britain was growing.

Joseph Hewes, who became John's friend in Philadelphia. Hewes was also a member of the committee that chose John to be an officer in the Continental Navy.

Two years earlier, the men of Boston had thrown a shipload of tea overboard to avoid paying the hated import tax. John realized that in such violent times the Continental Army would need a navy. He began to diligently study books on naval affairs.

Through his new friends, Jones met a young lady named Dorothea Dandridge and began courting her. Their feelings toward one another appeared to be mutual. Unfortunately, Dorothea's parents said the two could not marry. Because she was from a high-class family, Dorothea was expected to marry better. In 1777 she married Governor Patrick Henry of Virginia. Although John often talked of getting married and settling down, it never actually happened.

Joseph Hewes was now a member of the committee that established the navy and chose officers. Records show that on December 7, 1775, John Paul Jones was commissioned as a first lieutenant in the Continental Navy. To be commissioned in this navy meant he had completely separated himself from Britain— a very brave stand to take at that moment in history.

With ships such as this one, Britain had the
most powerful navy in the world. But George
Washington and John Paul Jones were
determined to build a strong navy that could
capture British ships and supplies.

Captain in the Continental Navy

The British Royal Navy was known around the world as the finest that ever sailed the seas. While some colonists felt that it was useless to raise up a navy to fight against the British, others felt it was important to have a Continental Navy. George Washington was one who agreed with John that the colonies must build a strong navy. A Continental Navy could capture British supply ships and take the needed supplies for the colonies' own army.

Early in the revolution, few colonists thought about independence. Instead, they thought they could convince King George III of Britain to give in to their demands. They believed that very soon the motherland and the colonies would once again live peacefully with one another. John, no doubt, wished the same. Then he could regain money due to him in London and in Tobago.

Aboard the ship *Alfred* as a lieutenant, John was put in full command until a captain arrived to take over. During the cold winter, when the Delaware River was blocked with ice, John had his men practice loading and shooting the cannons aboard. While on board the *Alfred,* John hoisted up the very first flag of freedom. This new Grand Union flag had 13 red and white stripes and the crosses of St. George and St. Andrew.

Once Commodore Hopkins arrived, his first orders were to sail to the Bahamas and capture British gunpowder and cannons at forts located there. Hopkins was in command of a small fleet of four ships. The mission was successful, and the fleet came home with British cannons, shells, fuses, gun carriages, and gunpowder.

The Grand Union flag, first raised by John as a lieutenant on the *Alfred*. The stripes stood for the 13 colonies. The crosses symbolized England and Scotland.

During this cruise, they encountered the HMS *Glasgow,* and a battle followed. Hopkins handled the encounter badly, yet he was later hailed by the press as a hero. John, on the lower deck with the men he'd trained, made a good showing. The *Glasgow* was badly damaged in this short battle, but John learned a great deal

Esek Hopkins, first commander of the Continental Navy. While serving under Hopkins, John and his men fought their first battle at sea.

about ship-to-ship combat.

In the spring of 1776 John was awarded temporary command of the **sloop** *Providence* as its captain. John's thinking about the relationship between America and Britain had by then changed. He knew that Americans really did want independence from Britain and that the Congress was serious about building a strong navy to fight the Revolutionary War.

John was happy with the sleek, fast-moving *Providence*. He could lead the enemy on a merry chase with it. On August 8, 1776, a month after the signing of the Declaration of Independence, John finally received a formal captain's commission from the Congress. This commission, he felt, should have been dated in May when the temporary commission of captain had been given to him. In spite of his letters of protest, his request was ignored. This difference of a few months put him lower in seniority than other, less-qualified officers. This upset John.

John and his sloop and crew of 75 were sent out with orders to "Seize, Take, Sink, Burn or Destroy that of our Enemys." As captain of this sloop of war, he was now completely in charge and free to show what he could do. During a six weeks' cruise, he and the crew successfully destroyed part of the British fishing fleet in Canada.

From there he went on to capture 16 enemy ships, which showed full proof of his abilities. He cleverly rescued another American warship from a large British **frigate**, then slipped away, racing the *Providence* to safety. One of the prizes John took during this cruise was the HMS *Mellish*. This ship's cargo included many cases of warm winter uniforms that had been intended for the British soldiers. The urgently needed supplies were quickly sent to George Washington's army.

When Congress published a new list of 24 naval captains, John was disappointed to see that he was number 18. This meant he had lost out on a chance to command a fleet. He wrote letters stating the unfairness of this rating, but the list was not changed. For the most part, John was unknown in the colonies. Most of the other officers had lived in America all their lives. They were well known and respected.

Looking back, this seems terribly unfair. However, it must be noted that John was the only man without local backing to ever receive command of a new ship. This tells us that the Congress did, in fact, trust him.

Neatness and appearance were of great importance to John. In March 1777 he met with a group of navy officers at Boston to discuss naval uniforms. They decided on a dress uniform of a dark blue coat with white linings and lapels and a stand-up collar. This was worn with a white waistcoat, breeches, and stockings. (Knee breeches were the mark of a gentleman and officer; crewmen wore long baggy trousers.) There were gold **epaulets** on the shoulders, gold buttons on the coat with embroidered buttonholes, and gold lace edging on the coat and waistcoat.

The Continental Congress had by this time given **privateers** permission to take any and all

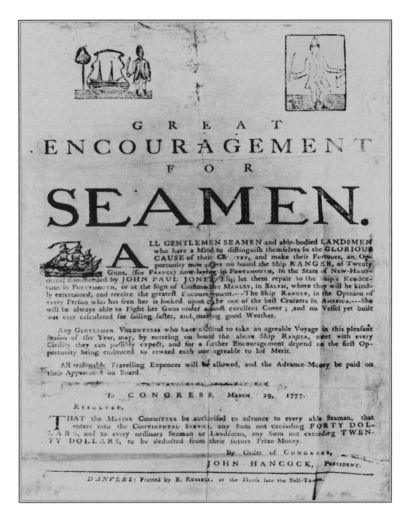

A 1777 poster recruiting volunteers in America to "make their fortunes" on John's ship, the *Ranger*.

enemy ships they possibly could. Privateers were allowed to keep all the money and goods they took from the British ships. This was not true for the naval crews. They were required to turn over a large percentage of their prizes to the Congress. This made it extremely difficult to round up a crew to serve in the navy. Men preferred to serve on privateer ships where they could make more money. John wrote many letters explaining the problems of this system and how it should be corrected. The Congress listened and, as a result, increased the captors' share from one-third to one-half. This did not solve the problem completely, but it was a step in the right direction.

June 14, 1777, was a famous day—the day that the new Stars and Stripes flag was adopted. It was also the day that the Continental Congress appointed Captain John Paul Jones to command the new frigate *Ranger.* The most exciting and dramatic phase of John's career was about to unfold.

John Paul Jones as captain of the *Ranger*. His daring missions would make him famous in Britain, France, and America.

"I Intend to Go in Harm's Way"

arlier in 1777, Captain Lambert Wickes was sent on a very important mission. Aboard his ship, *Reprisal*, he was to take Benjamin Franklin to France, where Franklin would serve as an American diplomat. The struggling new nation desperately needed help from France. Perhaps Franklin could convince the French to give aid and finances.

After leaving Franklin in France, Wickes went on to capture a great number of British ships. In a letter to Captain Wickes, members of the Continental Congress wrote: "Let Old England See how they like to have an active Enemy at their door, they have sent Fire and Sword to Ours."

An American privateer captain named Gustavus Conyngham roamed the coasts of Britain, France, and Spain in a 14-gun **cutter** named *Revenge.* In a period of 18 months he disabled nearly 60 British ships. The Americans were at last striking fear into the hearts of the British.

Benjamin Franklin was 70 years old when he sailed aboard the *Reprisal* to France as America's first foreign diplomat. This was a courageous thing to do. If the *Reprisal* had been captured by the British, Franklin could have been sentenced to be hanged for high treason. Franklin's work in France turned out to be very successful. In 1778 a Treaty of Alliance was signed between France and America. Without France's aid of ships, guns, soldiers, and finances, America might never have won the war for independence.

Sailing into this scene came John, aboard the *Ranger.* "I wish to have no Connection with any Ship that does not sail *fast,* for I intend *to go in harm's way*," he said. When he arrived in France, John immediately met with Benjamin Franklin, and the two soon became very close friends. In the future Franklin would always be

Benjamin Franklin in Paris. In honor of his friendship with Franklin, John named his French ship after Franklin's book *Poor Richard's Almanac*.

ready to give a word of support for John.

After wintering on the coasts of France and making repairs to the *Ranger,* John and his restless crew set off on a cruise that would make them famous. John had hoped that other French ships would go with him, but they did not. On April 10, 1778, the *Ranger* sailed up the Irish Sea toward waters that John knew well—the Solway Firth.

No American had yet attacked a British port, although the British had attacked and burned American towns. John wanted to be the first to **retaliate** and get even with the British. The crew members were more interested in attacking merchant ships than attacking a town on shore. They wanted the money from the ships.

The *Ranger* arrived at Whitehaven. This was the harbor John had left when he was 13 years old. He ordered two crewmen to go ashore in small boats. They were to take guns, burn ships, and destroy warehouses. Things did not go according to plan. Some of the crewmen wound up in a pub helping themselves to rum and ale. One crew member ran from house to house warning the people of the Americans' arrival. With the citizens alerted and rushing to defend their port, all John and his crew were able to do was dump over a barrel of tar and set fire to one ship. One thing was sure, however: John had terrorized the British Isles. There had not been a surprise attack on a British seaport since 1667.

Although John was disappointed in his failure to burn hundreds of ships in Whitehaven Harbor, he did not slow down. His next plan was to kidnap some rich person to hold hostage. This way the Americans could exchange the hostage for prisoners the British had taken. John was always concerned for these American prisoners and often wrote letters to Congress suggesting how their release might be obtained.

Across the Solway and further up the bay of Kirkcudbright was Selkirk castle. The Earl of Selkirk and his wife, Lady Selkirk, lived there. John may have seen or met this wealthy couple when he was a boy. Sighting the castle in the distance, he manned a small cutter and went ashore with a few of his men. The mission failed when they were informed by the butler that the earl was not at home.

John wanted to return to the cutter quickly.

Then his men reminded him that the crew had not gained any prizes. They asked permission to loot the house. Knowing that his refusal might cause resistance, John agreed. Several officers were allowed to enter the home and take only the family silver. This amounted to many expensive pieces, including a teapot that contained tea leaves still wet from the breakfast tea.

Lady Selkirk behaved herself in a dignified and calm manner, ordering the servants to collect all the silver and not to miss one piece. When John later heard of the courage of Lady Selkirk, he wrote her a long letter. In the letter he apologized and offered to buy back the silver and return it. After the war he did just that.

After making two land raids, the *Ranger* might have been expected to hurry off to safer waters. But John was not finished yet. He meant to take on the sloop *Drake,* which he'd seen at sea before he and his men attacked Whitehaven. He approached the ship without his colors flying. Captain Burden of the _Drake_ sent out a small boat called a gig to see what ship was nearing. John invited the lieutenant in the gig to board the _Ranger,_ and promptly told him he was a prisoner of the Continental Navy.

Raising the Stars and Stripes, John headed for deeper waters, tricking the _Drake_ into following. The battle between the two ships, which were evenly matched in size, lasted just over one hour. The captain of the _Drake_ was killed and the second officer badly wounded. The sails were torn and the rigging shot away. The third in command cried, "Quarters," which means they surrendered. On May 8 the _Drake,_ with the British flags flying upside down beneath the American flag, sailed in to Brest, France. There were 200 British prisoners on board.

After this success John hoped he finally would be put in command of a fleet of ships. His heart was set on attacking the British once again. He spoke to France's minister of marine, Gabriel de Sartine, asking for two or three frigates with which he could capture British ships the world over. The French at first agreed but later changed their minds. Desperate to have ships to command, John wrote to commissioners in France. He wrote to his friend Joseph Hewes back in America. He even wrote to the king of France. While these people got tired of so many letters, John's correspondence gives us a picture of his character. He was determined.

At last the French government bought a ship for John's use. But it was a merchant ship. John was responsible for fitting it out. In addition to getting the sails and rigging, he had to travel throughout France locating and buying guns and cannons. The *Duc de Duras* was a bigger, heavier ship than any of the ships John had commanded before. In honor of his friend Benjamin Franklin, John renamed the ship *Bonhomme Richard*, after Franklin's famous book called *Poor Richard's Almanac*.

Many of the crew members of the *Richard* were Americans who had been released from

Ships at battle on the rolling seas. France, Britain, and America all had ships roaming the ocean, seeking out and engaging the enemy.

British prisons. Some had been released due to John's efforts. The 20 officers were all aboard by choice. John had said, "I wish for none but volunteers who with all their hearts are determined to go with me anywhere and

A big, heavy ship like the *Bonhomme Richard*. John's flagship *Richard* led a fleet of seven French boats of different sizes.

everywhere in pursuit of honor." This was a crew of experienced seamen. It would turn out to be the best crew John ever commanded.

John's first lieutenant, Richard Dale, had escaped from a British prison. He was anxious to fight the British and even the score. While John was not close friends with any of his men or officers, he did respect Lieutenant Dale.

John's fleet consisted of the frigates *Alliance* and *Pallas,* the brig *Vengeance,* the cutter *Cerf,* and two privateers, the *Monsieur* and *Granville,* and of course, the *Bonhomme Richard.* All were under the command of French captains who had been given commissions in the American navy. All were ordered to pay close attention to signals from the **flagship**, *Bonhomme Richard.*

After many long months of waiting, John was now ready "to go in harm's way" with his very own fleet.

Captain Jones on a ship. He wanted to command the first American ship to attack a British port.

The Return of "Pirate" Jones

While John was pleased with the overall performance of his own ship and crew, he had some troubles with the rest of the French fleet. The captain of the *Alliance,* Pierre Landais, who had been in the French navy for many years, was not willing to take orders from John. As a result, Captain Landais caused John a great number of problems.

John's orders from France were to sail north of Britain and destroy as many merchant ships as possible along the way. On August 14, 1779, somewhere near the west coast of Ireland, John and his crew captured two brigs. The brigs were manned by "prize crews" from John's ship and sent back to France.

While all this was taking place, the captains of the other vessels paid no attention to John's signals. They went after other British merchant ships on their own and rejoined John's fleet whenever they pleased. This frustrated John, but there was nothing he could do about it.

Not long thereafter, the two privateers left the fleet altogether, and the cutter went back to France because of difficulties in high seas. The size of John's fleet became much smaller with the loss of these ships.

John was determined to capture British ships and continued on his way, taking prizes as he went. At Cape Wrath, at the northwest point of Scotland, they captured the *Union*. This British ship was filled with clothing for the British army in Canada. John gave Captain Landais the privilege of manning the *Union*, even though Landais had no real part in the ship's

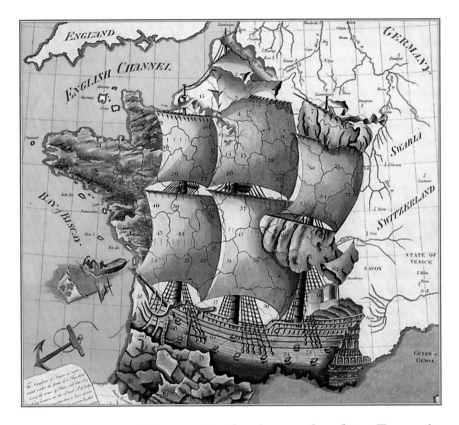

A map of France in the form of a ship. France's support of the colonies, and its provisions of ships and supplies, were crucial to America's final victory in the Revolutionary War.

capture. But Landais was still upset and continued to ignore John's signals and orders. When John sent men aboard the *Alliance* to confer with Landais, the French captain spoke of John in highly disrespectful terms. Later

John ordered Landais to come aboard the flagship for a conference. The uncooperative French captain refused.

As John's small fleet continued southward along the west coast of Scotland, the citizens of Scotland were in a panic. The much-feared Pirate Paul Jones, as they called him, had returned! People along the shores packed up their families and possessions and left their houses. Ships anchored along the coast quickly moved into hidden coves and safer harbors. John's ship came within a cannon shot of the town of Leith, but a strong wind arose and he had to move out to sea again.

On September 23, while at sea, John came upon a **convoy** of 42 merchant ships that was protected by the HMS *Serapis* (Se-ray-pis) and the HMS *Countess of Scarborough*. The *Serapis* was a large, copper-bottomed frigate. The copper sheets fastened to the bottom helped her sail faster. She had 50 guns and a well-trained crew of 300 sailors. Captain Richard

Pearson of the *Serapis* had been warned that John was in the area and therefore was already expecting him.

Captain Jones had always wanted to capture an entire convoy, but he knew he would have to sink the heavily-armed escorts first. At 6:00 P.M. the *Richard* set flag signals for John's fleet to form a line of battle. With all his fleet shooting together, he thought, they could sink the escorts and take the convoy without too much difficulty. Unfortunately, none of the other ships obeyed his orders. John and his crew were left all alone. Never one to back down from a fight, John ordered his ship forward, and they sailed on toward the *Serapis.*

By this time, drummers were beating a **tattoo**, which told the gun crews to get ready. The seas were calm with a few light breezes blowing. The crew sloshed the decks with water to keep them from catching fire. Gunners were at their battle stations, and sharpshooters climbed into the riggings where they could aim down on the *Serapis.* Young boys, called powder monkeys, ran back and forth piling cartridges of gunpowder near the gun crews.

By 6:30 P.M. the sun had gone down, and a soft harvest moon was shining on the waters. Soon the British captain hailed the *Richard.* John sent up the Stars and Stripes flag and ordered his men to begin firing. Almost at the same time, the *Serapis* fired off a number of its big cannons. John would later write, "The battle being thus begun was Continued with Unremitting fury."

When the big old cannons on the *Richard* were fired, some of them exploded, killing or wounding the gun crews and setting fires on the deck. John knew he could not win by means of the big guns. He would have to rely on grenades and his sharpshooters.

The night grew darker and the fires and explosions of guns and cannons lit up the sky. Hundreds of citizens came out to the cliffs of

Flamborough Head to watch the spectacular scene. Word had spread quickly that the feared pirate was cornered. They wanted to see him destroyed.

The two ships moved around in the water, with each crew attempting to board the enemy ship. At John's order "Boarders away," the crew tried to board the *Serapis* but were driven back by the British sailors. John turned his ship to move it into a better position. The guns from the *Serapis* pounded the *Richard,* creating large, gaping holes in its side.

Captain Pearson of the *Serapis* now moved to force his ship ahead. He hoped to turn his ship across the bow of the *Richard* and sweep her with gunfire. Instead the two ships moved so closely together that they crashed into one another. Sure the *Richard* was badly damaged, Pearson called out, "Has your ship struck?" This was another way of asking John if he was ready to surrender yet. John hollered back, his famous reply, "I have not yet begun to fight!"

The ships parted and sailed side by side, exchanging **broadside** attacks. As the *Serapis* began to pull ahead, Pearson lowered the top-sails to decrease speed and stay within range. Just then a slight breeze came up and drove the *Richard* ahead of the other vessel. John then attempted to cross the bow of the *Serapis,* but the rigging and sails were so damaged, the *Richard* again crashed into the other ship.

The front of the *Serapis* was now tangled in the rigging on the rear of the *Richard.* The wind in the sails caused the two ships to move until they were again side by side—bow to stern and stern to bow. All tied together, and being pushed around by the wind, the two ships came together so tightly that the muzzles of the cannons from both ships were touching each other.

This was a strange situation, but one that John liked. The American captain knew his only chance of victory was to disable the rigging of the *Serapis* and kill off her crew. The *Richard*

The battle with the *Serapis*. Tangled up and lashed together much of the time, the two ships pounded each other unmercifully.

had no cannons left. The determined John helped his men drag a nine-pounder cannon from the **port** side, then assisted in firing it at the *Serapis* as the battle raged on.

Cries from the dying and wounded sounded out amidst the crack of gunfire and the deep rumble of the big cannons. Blood ran on the decks and fires broke out here and there. As the *Richard* took on water and began to slowly sink, men furiously manned the pumps to keep it afloat.

Down in the hold of the *Richard,* 200 British prisoners were panicking at the thought of drowning. John ordered all of the prisoners to be released to help man the pumps. This wise maneuver freed his men to return to the battle, where they were desperately needed.

John's "topmen" were excellent marksmen and were able to pick off most of the British gunners with amazing accuracy. One very brave sailor, a Scot named William Hamilton, volunteered to carry a bucket of grenades and a live match and crawl out on the damaged **yardarm**. The yardarm was now hanging over the deck of the *Serapis.* Hamilton dropped a lit grenade into an open hatch, which exploded powder cartridges aboard the *Serapis*. The resulting explosion killed at least 20 men. John continued to fire at the enemy's mainmast in order to disable the *Serapis*.

It was just after 10:00 P.M. and the situation seemed hopeless for the *Richard*. The fires burned out of control, and the ship was still sinking. All cannons were silent except for three, and the officers and crew were weary and losing heart.

Then, it is said, that one of John's crew attempted to pull down the *Richard*'s flag to signal a surrender. John ordered him to stop immediately, but he would not. This was an act of mutiny punishable by death. John raised his pistol and shot the man in the head.

Any lesser man would have given up by this time, but not John. The enemy may have had a bigger ship, more men, and more guns, but John had the grit to refuse to give up. He fought on with ferocious determination and an unwillingness to accept defeat. At about

During the battle with the *Serapis*, John was said to have shot a sailor who was trying to pull down the *Richard*'s flag.

10:30 P.M. Pearson, knowing it was he who must surrender, hauled down the **ensign** with his own hands. The long battle was finally over.

John and the *Richard* had received no help at all from the other ships in the fleet during the entire battle. In fact, at one point Captain Landais brought the *Alliance* into the area and began firing on the *Richard*! Landais was later punished for his actions. Meanwhile, to her credit, the smaller French ship *Pallas* and her brave crew forced the other British escort ship, *Countess,* to surrender after a long and fierce struggle.

After the historic battle between the *Bonhomme Richard* and the *Serapis,* many stories and songs about John spread quickly. One ballad went like this:

You have heard o' Paul Jones?

Have you not? Have you not?

How he came to Leith Pier, and he fill'd the folks with fear,

And he fill'd the folks with fear,

Did he not?

He took the *Serapis*

Did he not? Did he not?

He took the *Serapis,* tho' the battle it was hot;

But a rogue and vagabond,

Is he not?

At the moment of surrender, Lieutenant Dale boarded the *Serapis* to escort Captain Pearson over to the *Richard.* The two captains went to John's wrecked cabin and had a friendly glass of wine.

Great ships on fire. Although John's ship won the battle with the *Serapis*, the *Richard* could not be saved and sank the next day.

Forgotten
Hero

The battle had lasted for hours. It was the first time an American naval vessel had taken so great a British warship. For decades Britain had ruled the seas, but that was changing.

For an entire day the survivors of *Richard's* crew fought the fires and tried to save the old ship. John gave orders for the carpenters to keep making repairs, and for others to keep the pumps going. At the same time, surgeons worked on the wounded, and the dead were given proper sea burials.

Then, on September 24th, John ordered all the wounded to be transferred to the other ships of the fleet. He could see his ship was beyond saving. It was with great sadness that he watched her sink beneath the waters of the North Sea.

John returned to France as a conquering hero. Honors were heaped upon him and he enjoyed the attention a lot. Benjamin Franklin wanted John to sail to America right away with a supply of **muskets** and cloth for uniforms for the Americans. After all, the fight for freedom was still raging back in the colonies.

John did not want to go back right away. He was still trying to get money due him and his crew for back pay from the Congress. While in France John spent time courting beautiful ladies and enjoying the wealthy society of Paris. King Louis XVI presented him with a sword that was inscribed to the man who defended the "Freedom of the Seas." Another honor from the king was to invest John with the Order of Military Merit. This allowed him to use the title "Chevalier," which he sometimes used to sign his name. At the king's request, a

**King Louis XVI of France, who awarded
John the Order of Military Merit in
honor of his victories over the British.**

noted French sculptor cast a very beautiful
marble bust of John. John was extremely
proud of the statue and had copies made to
give to his friends.

It wasn't until 1781 that he finally returned to America. This time he was captain of the *Ariel*. In Philadelphia he answered questions from the Continental Congress regarding his actions while away. His written answers were so detailed and thorough that the Congress voted a formal resolution of thanks to John for his outstanding service to the cause. Then they awarded him command of a new ship named *America*. Excitedly he traveled to Portsmouth to fit out his ship.

By this time, however, the war was coming to an end. When General Cornwallis surrendered to George Washington at Yorktown, the Revolutionary War was over. The Congress now felt there was no need for a navy and gave the

John was overcome with joy over the sword presented to him by Louis XVI. The handle was adorned with figures from Greek mythology as well as flags, floral designs, and dolphins. After John died, the sword passed through several hands but finally was given to Captain Richard Dale, one of John's old shipmates. Later, one of Dale's descendants lent it to the Naval Academy. It was then placed near John's tomb, where it remains today.

America to France. This was a bitter disappointment to John, and it left him with no ship to command. He had always longed to be admiral of an entire fleet. But chances of that happening were more remote than ever.

Though the war was over, John encouraged the Congress to build up a proper navy and to create schools where junior officers could be taught. He also favored the use of signal flags, which would reduce errors in communication between ships. But at the time, America had many other more important things to think about besides a navy. Many of John's recommendations did come to pass, but not until many years after his death.

After the Congress paid him a settlement for his services, John decided to return to Paris. A warm reception was always waiting for him there. While in Paris he learned that Catherine the Great, the empress of Russia, wanted him to help the Russian navy fight the Turks in the Black Sea. This was his chance at last.

When he arrived in St. Petersburg on May 2, 1788, he was named Rear Admiral John Paul Jones. He was to sail in the flagship *Vladimir.* But instead of being in command of an entire fleet, he was put in joint command with another Russian officer, Prince Potemkin. Potemkin wrote unfair reports about John and sent them to the empress. Because Potemkin was a favorite of hers, Catherine believed him rather than the American. The Russian sailors, however, respected John and fought well under his leadership.

After many misunderstandings and many unhappy days in the country, John was given two years' leave of absence from the Russian navy. Although he kept hoping he would be called back to take over an important command, it never happened. John never saw Russia again.

In 1790 he returned to Paris. Around this time John toyed with the idea of returning to America to purchase land near Lancaster, Pennsylvania. At age 43, perhaps he would find a quiet farm and settle down. But his hope of being called into service in Russia held him in Europe.

Life in Paris, meanwhile, had changed. The people were ready to overthrow the king. Many of John's old friends had fled the city in fear for their lives. John's health was failing. His hair had turned gray, he suffered from a wheezing cough, and his legs were painfully swollen. He felt betrayed and forgotten.

Back in America, John was not totally forgotten, however. Together, George Washington and Thomas Jefferson had decided to appoint John as a commissioner to Algiers. There he would work to free American prisoners and to set up a treaty with that country. If John had known of this appointment, he would have been very pleased. But sadly, the dispatch did not leave America until mid-July. John died on July 18, 1792. He was 45 years old.

John was buried in a cemetery outside of Paris that was especially for foreigners who were Protestants. There his body stayed until 1905, when it was returned to the United States with full honors. President Theodore Roosevelt sent four cruisers to France to escort the naval hero's body home.

A formal and elaborate ceremony was held at Annapolis, Maryland, home of the United States Naval Academy. The Naval Academy was based on the principles John proposed more than 150 years earlier. He was finally laid to rest in an ornate grave patterned after the great tomb of Napoleon. John's tomb is located in the Naval Academy Chapel.

Although John was a very complicated man and sometimes quite difficult to understand, he was fearless in battle, and more at home on the high seas

In 1898, General Horace Porter was ambassador to France. He began the search to find the grave of John Paul Jones. Since city buildings had been built over the suspected spot, the search took five years. When at last the grave was discovered, it was found that Jones's body had been well preserved with alcohol and carefully packed in straw. The considerate French had packed it so the body could travel safely across the ocean.

New graduates of the U.S. Naval Academy fling their hats into the air. The Naval Academy still uses ideas that John proposed over 150 years ago.

than on land. He had wise insight as to how a navy should be set up, and how it should be operated. The passing of time proved him to be right. Many of his ideas were later adopted and are still in use today in the U.S. navy.

GLOSSARY

apprentice–a person learning a trade from a skilled worker

barrell staves–narrow strips of iron or wood that form the sides and lining of a ship

bow–the forward part of a ship

brig–a two-masted, square-rigged sailing ship

broadside–a firing of all the guns on one side of a warship

brogue–a strong regional accent

bulwarks–the parts of a ship's sides that are above the upper deck

cat-o'-nine-tails–a whip made of nine lines or chords attached to a handle

convoy–a group of ships organized to sail together for protection

cutter–a kind of fast, single-masted sailing vessel

ensign–a national flag or banner displayed on ships

epaulets–a shoulder ornament on certain military dress uniforms

flagship–a ship bearing the flag of a fleet commander

frigate–a fast, square-rigged warship

muskets–large guns used before the invention of the rifle

pig iron–crude iron

port–the left-hand side of a ship, facing forward

privateer–a ship privately owned but used by a government during wartime

retaliate–to pay back for an injury

rogue–a mischievous person; scamp

sloop–a one-masted boat with rigging on the front and back

starboard–the right-hand side of a ship, facing forward

stern–the back part of a ship

tattoo–a signal sounded on a drum or bugle to call men to their posts

vagabond–a tramp or wanderer

yardarm–either end of the yard of a square-rigged ship

CHRONOLOGY

1747   Born John Paul on July 6 in Kirkcudbright, Scotland.

1761   Apprenticed aboard the brig *Friendship*.

1764   Signs on the *King George*, a slave-trade ship, for two years.

1769   Becomes captain of brig *John*.

1770   Is arrested in Scotland for murder; inducted into Masonic Lodge in Kirkcudbright.

1772   Kills a mutinous sailor and is forced to flee for his life; changes his name to John Paul Jones; goes into hiding.

1774   Arrives in Virginia.

1775   Moves to Philadelphia; is commissioned first lieutenant in the Continental Navy.

1776   Is commissioned captain by the Continental Congress.

1777   Is given command of the *Ranger*; sails to France.

1778   Raids Whitehaven; *Ranger* becomes first American vessel to capture British man-of-war, HMS *Drake*.

1779   Receives command of *Bonhomme Richard*; engages in battle with *Serapis* on September 23.

1781   Returns to Philadelphia; the Revolutionary War ends.

1788   Becomes rear admiral in Russia under Catherine the Great.

1790   Returns to and stays in Paris.

1792   Dies in Paris at age 45; buried in small private ceremony.

1905   Body is escorted back to America and laid to rest at the United States Naval Academy in Annapolis, Maryland.

REVOLUTIONARY WAR TIME LINE

1765 The Stamp Act is passed by the British. Violent protests against it break out in the colonies.

1766 Britain ends the Stamp Act.

1767 Britain passes a law that taxes glass, painter's lead, paper, and tea in the colonies.

1770 Five colonists are killed by British soldiers in the Boston Massacre.

1773 People are angry about the taxes on tea. They throw boxes of tea from ships in Boston harbor into the water. It ruins the tea. The event is called the Boston Tea Party.

1774 The British pass laws to punish Boston for the Boston Tea Party. They close Boston harbor. Leaders in the colonies meet to plan a response to these actions.

1775 The battles of Lexington and Concord begin the American Revolution.

1776 The Declaration of Independence is signed. France and Spain give money to help the Americans fight Britain. Nathan Hale is captured by the British. He is charged with being a spy and is executed.

1777 Leaders choose a flag for America. The American troops win some important battles over the British. General Washington and his troops spend a very cold, hungry winter in Valley Forge.

1778 France sends ships to help the Americans win the war. The British are forced to leave Philadelphia.

1779 French ships head back to France. The French support the Americans in other ways.

1780 Americans discover that Benedict Arnold is a traitor. He escapes to the British. Major battles take place in North and South Carolina.

1781 The British surrender at Yorktown.

1783 A peace treaty is signed in France. British troops leave New York.

1787 The U.S. Constitution is written. Delaware becomes the first state in the Union.

1789 George Washington becomes the first president. John Adams is vice president.

FURTHER READING

Carse, Robert. *Ports of Call.* New York: Scribners, 1967.

Fisher, Leonard Everett. *Stars & Stripes: Our National Flag.* New York: Holiday House, 1993.

Miller, Nathan. *The U.S. Navy, A History.* New York: William Morrow, 1990.

Morrison, Samuel Eliot. *John Paul Jones, A Sailor's Biography.* Boston: Little, Brown and Company, 1959.

Nickles, Greg. *Pirates.* New York: Crabtree Publishing, 1997.

Ronald, Susan. *France, the Crossroads of Europe.* Parsippany, NJ: Dillon Press, 1998.

Taylor-Wilkie, Doreen. *Scotland.* Austin, TX: Steck-Vaughn, 1991.

Walsh, John Evangelist. *Night on Fire.* New York: McGraw-Hill Inc., 1978.

INDEX

PICTURE CREDITS

ABOUT THE AUTHOR

NORMA JEAN LUTZ, who lives in Tulsa, Oklahoma, has been writing professionally since 1977. She is the author of more than 250 short stories and articles as well as 36 books—fiction and nonfiction. Of all the writing she does, she most enjoys writing children's books.

Senior Consulting Editor **ARTHUR M. SCHLESINGER, JR.** is the leading American historian of our time. He won the Pulitzer Prize for his book *The Age of Jackson* (1945), and again for *A Thousand Days* (1965). This chronicle of the Kennedy Administration also won a National Book Award. He has written many other books, including a multi-volume series, *The Age of Roosevelt.* Professor Schlesinger is the Albert Schweitzer Professor of the Humanities at the City University of New York, and has been involved in several other Chelsea House projects, including the Colonial Leaders series of biographies on the most prominent figures of early American history.